Heart Without a Beat

A book of poems

A.W. Sandy

Dedication

To Mr. Santin:

Thank you for the positive vibes and the wholesome laughs in creative writing, 2011. I was just in grade 11, and I had no way of knowing the impact of your lessons until I got older. I've never forgotten you. Blessings!

~Andrea Williams-Sandy~

Table of Contents

Heart Without a Beat

A Book of Poems

A.W. Sandy

Always

down the broken road, I ride

with my broken heart

away in my broken car

tears falling freely

freely leaving my eyes as I ask God

WHY.

why did you leave?

you used to sit with me

on the beach, OUR beach

in our favorite shady part

and we used to speak of the future our future together

together forever

but...

but where did you go?

I want you back

because the guy you hate the most is trying
to get with me

and I don't think you'd like that

you wouldn't want that if you were still here

and it's all very difficult without you

what happened to always?

Apart of him

it's always been my dream

to find somebody that I could

thoroughly relate to

and I found him

he's beyond sexy

he's beyond beautiful

he's the one I've been waiting for

he's **mine**.

it's not fair for me to see him every day

and not being able to be a part of his life

to be with him, always

because where does that place me?

like prickly thorns on a dark wildflower

it hurts

it hurts to be away from him

it's totally not fair for him

to see me every day, and not have the courage

to say anything to me

so it has to be me

but I don't mind

because as long as I'm near him

I'm okay

he's okay

we both are living life if we have each other

we are both happy

I am a part of him

Blow

watch out, or I'll break your face

break your chin

your legs

and everything in between

you don't want to get on my bad side

because I've already had enough

enough of the lying

I've done enough crying to fill an empty lake

I don't think you understand

the severity of the situation

my heart is beating so fast

and look, the rain is falling

and it's thundering out there

but that is mild when it's in comparison

to what I'm feeling

a thousand firearms are blasting through my body

blood flying in every direction

my body goes numb

blink once

blink twice

I fall to the ground, and I take you down with me

jaw wrenching, spine breaking

paralyzed babe, we are both paralyzed

I struggle to regain strength

dark blood travels out of my mouth

and I take a firearm that's close by me

and I aim it at you

you whisper no

but I pull the trigger

I had enough

I walk away, with new power

I did it

Blow

Breaking Point

my insides are raging

hotter than lava

hotter than that fireball in the sky

hotter than I thought you were

why oh why did I let myself fall for you

to your little acts

sweet moments that made me feel so good

so good, it's indescribable

unbearable

intolerable, baby

why did you do it

I understand that you wanted me badly

I know you can't control your urges

but babe, why did you have to push me

push me to my breaking point

you know that I am vulnerable

gullible

absentminded

oblivious

so why did you implement those thoughts in my head why
did I weaken under your presence

why do you love torturing me

do you like seeing me broken

you're just sick

but guess what babe

I'm ready to hit the road

~ 7 ~

Breathe

as you took your last breath

my mind went somewhere

I couldn't believe

what I was seeing

you looked so pained

with your hair now untidy

with your lips that you once kissed me with

why?

what did I do

I took you for granted

you were just amazing

and I fell for you fast

I knew we shouldn't have gone into that abandoned house

with its rickety staircase

we ran up those juvenile, conniving stairs together

clowning around

what a stupid idea for Halloween night

and we reached the platform together

and I left the house crying alone

because amidst all that laughter

you slipped and fell down those stairs

the symbol of death

I shrieked loudly and ran after you

and your head was bleeding

I placed my head on your chest, I heard no heartbeat

I put my bloody hand into a fist

and I cried till the tears stopped flowing

the moon was shining way too brightly

I stood up, walked up those stairs, and jumped

but survived

I wanted to be with you

you always knew what to do and how to do it

but that night, I forgot how to breathe

anyway, it's too late, for both of us

Choice

it's up to you

what do you want to do

you decide

where do you want to go

how long do you want to be there

do you want me to be there with you?

baby, you can start by taking that shirt off

because it's getting a bit hot

and you can lay on my bed

I give you permission

you can kiss me on the lips

if that's what your heart desires

I'll just take off my shoes

and plop right beside you

since that's what I want

and I'll kiss your lips and neck

till it feels right, till dawn breaks

cuz that's what I want to do

I'll tell you everything is great, even when it's not

you don't have to play this game

I realize it's always been about you

I don't have any say

when it's all over, you'll be sorry

I'm calling the shots because the sky's the fucking limit

so I get outta my bed, tell you to put your shirt back on

undo those kisses, tell you to get the hell out of my house

it's my choice to leave you

it's my decision to leave your inconsiderate ass

I have the last say

and I'm saying bye

Cold

her disheveled hair covers her eyes

dark clothing covers her limp body

who is she?

the girl that everybody looks away from

the girl that cuts herself because she is hurting

the girl who gets frequent beatings

from her "mom" and "dad"

why must this happen to her?

the life of a drug addict

smoking blunts on Third street

losing herself

her eyes get heavy, her heart is black

she feels no remorse for what she does

ran away from that hell house

ran away from it all

her hands shake vigorously

whenever she lights a cigarette

a disgusting reminder of who she became

a fucking demon, she says

a fucking monster, they call her

she lights the cigarette

shuts the world out

shuts the universe out, just like they shut her out

bitches.

if her "mom" and "dad" hated her so much

why did they give her a name?

Courtney Anderson

she ditches the cigarette after taking one final puff

spits on the ground and sticks up her middle finger

to the sky

cursing whatever is up

there it's so incredibly disappointing to her

that the world

is so cold

Why

could you tell me why

I should believe what you say

you are a filthy liar

I hate when you act that way

I hate when you treat me

with such cruelty and pain

that in the end all I do

is lose more than I should gain.

there are no ifs, and, or buts

babe, you're all on your own

we used to be together, and item! but now look

you stand alone

being alone is such a creepy

feeling so creepy, I hide under the covers

you wouldn't have to be alone if you and I were still lovers

I could care less if you're gorgeous or not

it doesn't really matter to me

I just hope in the future, you'll open your eyes

wide enough, so you can see

and I loved you so badly, you'll never really know

but I shouldn't cry, no I shouldn't fret for you have a long
way to go

Granted

she loved him more than she could say

and he knew that

but ignored it

she was always getting played

she was infatuated with the guy

would do anything for his tricky ass

he had class

she couldn't deny

fucked her maybe twice a week if she was lucky

held on to him like a rubber ducky

the future was looking meek

the girl's friends tried to warn her she couldn't care less

she knew that one thing was for sure

he was obviously the best

the guy kicked her ass more than once

she was blinded by love

he classified her as a useless dunce

as the sky was getting darker above

Together

we made it, look

look at all we've done it's true when they say

two heads are better than one

baby, we have captured the essence of our dreams

to turn them into a reality

we did all of this together babe, we've beaten Goliath

the ultimate face-off

we took him DOWN, and we did it with pride

we gotta be strong, only the strong survive

we have to smile together because we made it

together we did

there is not one thing in this world

that I would trade to take your place

because you are sublime in every way

in my eyes, you shine brighter than all the stars

in the sky

and I love you more than I can express or say

togetherness is bliss in my eyes and when I'm away from
you, it's agonizing

you and I do wonders and that's all there is to the story

That Sucks

I swear

every time I see his face all I see is RED

because I don't like him

nothing about that fiend is likable

and he knows that

and I could fucking care less because he used me

played with my heart like a yo-yo

held me with a threatening grasp like a young child

handling a precious toy

he should get a taste of his own medicine which he will

but I won't induce it because I don't like him

and like I said, he knows that, so I won't fuck around

and neither should he, he should stop if he knows

what's good for him

so I'll let somebody else let him know what's up

I can't take it

his heart beats faster than a bullet piercing the sky

this happens when I'm near, he feels me, but guess what

I don't care, and it's so sad

Loneliness is the only commonality we share

Mommy Told Me

mommy told me I could be everything good

she used big words like wonderful and fabulous

mommy told me I was the prettiest creature

she ever had the pleasure to encounter

I never understood that fully, but I knew it was something
good

mommy told me I could soar higher than all the birds

if I wanted to

I knew that wasn't possible physically, but soar, I did

mommy told me Daddy left because he "couldn't take it
anymore"... I cried for long hours, for I had understood

mommy told me she would never leave me, ever

of course, she wouldn't leave me, I needed her

mommy started to get very sick, I saw terrible changes

I saw her lose clumps of hair, she got skinnier every day

mommy told me she got cancer, a terrible disease

I felt bad for her, but I tried to help her get better

mommy told me she would have to go to the hospital, and
fast

so I got on my galoshes, got my raincoat,

brought my faith along

mommy looked helpless on that day, all her hair gone I sat
by her bed, holding her hand, squeezing it tightly, sobbing

mommy passed away on October 3rd

two days before my birthday

I cried and cried, she told me she WOULD NEVER LEAVE

Before she died, she said to me:

Mackenzie, I am so sorry. I love you with all my heart

That was the very last thing mommy told me

Hidden

they look past me

it's like I'm not there

it's almost crazy

I feel paranoid

I don't know why

what do I have to do to be accepted

it's unfair, show your true face tell me what you want

I feel the negative vibe that you're giving me

I feel like crying no seriously, I do

there are no ifs, and, or buts

why do you treat me like that I would really like to know

you have the audacity to forget about me

you can see the pain in my eyes

you can see my tear-stricken cheeks

you can look at me and tell that I am hurting

wipe off my tears kiss them away, as you used to do

you wanna tell me something? tell me that you're sorry for
all the pain that you have caused me

I'm almost gone

Actually, I'm very far away

The One

I had to cherish the moment

I knew it would never last

how do you do it every time

I see you and my heart stops happiness is all I feel

when I'm with you

I'm so happy I had a chance to be with you

humorous, sympathetic, thoughtful in every way

you and I got it in the bag and together, we made it

weird power of love don't quite understand

how it works

the apple of my eye the love of my life

the air that I breathe I need you

hugged you as my life depended on your presence

as the sun is to the earth, I am to you

riches and gold are nothing compared

to the wealth of true love that we both share

and now

I miss you

I'm lost without you

like an infant without its blanket

I no longer feel safe

like a willow tree

with its branches and leaves blowing viciously in the wind

I have no sense of direction like a highway with no cars

I have nowhere to go you leave me in awe and still

to this very day, I could never forget

no, I must never forget the day

that you went away

What Lies Beneath

I don't care about the glitter or the glamour

or the fucking fame

all I care about is being next to you

in your arms

everything about you is sublime

amazing

marvellously incredible

I don't care if you have a pretty car or a pretty house

or lots of friends

all I care about is your smile

wakes me up in the middle of the night

keeps me secure

I don't care where you're going

where you came from

or where you are in your life right now

as long as I am with you every step of the way

everything I need and want, is right here in front of me
everything good comes from you

as the sun is to the earth

I am to you

that will never change

and when we are old and still deeply in love

we will sit on our front porch

recalling our youthful days

you and I will look deep into each other's eyes

shed happy tears and say in unison

"Aren't you happy we both went for what lies beneath?"

Nothing speaks louder.

Alone

being alone is sheer solitude

as I walked home from school my mind raced

I just couldn't wait to see the look on my mom's face

and my sisters as well

I had gotten an A+ on my science project I felt great

I approached my house and was about to ring

the doorbell

when I noticed the door was open a crack and my jaw

fell to the floor and my eyebrows went to the sky

why was the door left open? and I was afraid to enter

but I did anyway and I pushed the door

and it creaked a sound I never recognized

from that door

my heart was running away from me

I climbed the stairs to my living room the lights were dim
the air has a chill, the window was open

and there was a silence

I looked all around me strained to hear voices

but nothing

there was nothing

I climbed up the next flight of stairs to my kitchen

and it was brighter there, and the breeze was calm

but fear got the best of me

I called for my mom, I called for my sisters

no answer

what's a 7-year-old to think?

coming home from school and your family

has evaporated from the world

I mean what's a 7-year-old supposed to do

after a life of being surrounded by hundreds of people

still feeling so isolated

I felt queasy instantly and tears stung my eyes

anger seeped through me I threw my backpack

on the floor

I, being terribly distraught, threw myself on the floor
maybe I knew too much

maybe I was too mature for my age

mothers and sisters should never leave

why was I left here I wanted my mom

to be proud of my mark

I wanted to instigate sibling rivalry and rub my A+ all up
in their faces out of fun

but they weren't here, and I cried but decided that since I
was at home ALL ALONE, I might as well eat, and I went
to the fridge gripping the handle and

I saw the note

Rise

they called him a freak

they ruined his life

made him feel useless

couldn't take it anymore

working in a soup shop- his only job

the only way to get away from it all

how frightful he was

of his life

his family turned him away

how he cried

what a life to live

he was a handsome guy a straight-A student

he had it going for him

the words people said to him hurt

eventually, he stopped going to school

and when he saw his friends, graduating being successful
he saw red

but he asked for it when

he passed by the Victorian-style school

the kids called him

old boy!

he felt like a piece of junk

he rushed past his favorite alleyway the place

that made him feel serene

but he shivers to himself, how cold he felt

how he held himself in the face of society

how low he was, compared to most

but like the sun peeking up over the horizon one day, he
too would rise above all